WORTHY

By: Jill Rohrbaugh

D1559633

WELCOME!

Grab your favorite cup of coffee, a pen. Open up your heart as you open up this book. It's time to get free and allow God to do "a great work" in you. Jill Rohrbaugh A Women's Devotional to "Worthy"

"Worthy"

A 3 Week Transformational Devotional to the Life God Wants for You

By:
Jill Rohrbaugh and the Holy Spirit

This book goes out to my dad. The first person I ever got to watch cling to Jesus and never let go.

About the Writer

Jill Rohrbaugh

Jill grew up in Baltimore, Maryland in a loving home with wonderful parents and two siblings. After taking a dark road in her early 20's, she was on the path of destruction but Jesus saved her. She has since moved to Pennsylvania to marry the love she waited for. She has 3 amazing stepchildren and 2 of her own with her husband Neil. She would say the song "Amazing Grace" was the story of her life.

<u>Inspiration</u>

This book was inspired by the book "Add More -ing to Your Life" By: Gabby Bernstien. When I was just starting my journey to Christ, I read this book. While it isn't a Christian Book, I'll never forget the impact it had on me. Once I matured a bit as a Christ Follower, I told myself I needed to write something like it, but for Christians. I can only pray that the vision I have to turn people to Christ through this book will be a reality some day. It's my greatest privilege to know Christ and lead others to do the same.

<u>Preface</u>

I grew up knowing the phrase, "when the student is ready the teacher appears." I just never knew the impact that that truth would have on me one day.

It took years, but finally I realized that my Teacher had been there all along waiting for me. It was not until I had taken every dark road that I, (the student) was ready. And when I was, it felt like the hero I had been waiting for all my life showed up like all those love stories I watched all those lonely nights.

Friends, God is always pursuing us. He wants all of us. But it is not until we make the choice to want Him back that we will clearly see His way. And His way is the way of the Spirit. Letting the Spirit lead brings "love, joy, peace, patience, kindness, goodness, gentleness, faithfulness, and self-control." -Galatians 5:22-23. *And who wouldn't want that?*

I am happy to say that if you are here, then you are ready to receive the message from the greatest teacher who ever walked the earth. For the next 3 weeks we are going to let go of all our old ways and let the Lord "transform us and renew our minds. Then you will be able to test and approve what God's will is- His good, pleasing and perfect Will."- Romans 12:2

So, let's get started, shall we?

Introduction

I'm so excited that you decided to go on this journey. The purpose of this devotional is to light up the dark places you've been fearful to address. It's not going to be easy work but it will be well worth it and lead you to knowing in Christ you are WORTHY!

The plan: This is 3 weeks of deep intentional work. You get the weekends off but that doesn't mean you stop using the things you've learned from the week. In fact, each weekend is time for you to take what you've discovered, reflect on it and apply it! Each day you will read the devotional and then dig into the work. After the work for the day, we will pray over what we did.

At the end, God will get all the glory and you will be ready to face everyday in a new and wonderful way. I can't wait for us to begin!

TABLE OF CONTENTS

<u>Week 1</u>

Day 1
Surrender to Him

On the day of my 31st Birthday, I cried from the time I got up 'til the time I went to bed. Since the age of 20 I had cycled through one relationship to the next. Most of them extremely unhealthy and others verbally and physically abusive. On my 31st birthday I was still in a relationship that I had been in for two years and knew in my heart it was not the relationship God wanted for me. I was new at being a Christ follower at that time and the Holy Spirit seemed closer than ever. I couldn't ignore the nudge the Spirit was giving me. I needed to face my past to have the life God wanted for me. It was going to be painful. I had suppressed so much for years. Digging all that up and facing it for the first time was the scariest thing I'd ever done. Yes, even scarier than being threatened and abused. It's crazy how much we fear our own emotions. We go to great lengths not to *feel*. This is a brilliant tactic of the devil. He schemes to make us think it would be too hard to go *through the pain* so instead we do all we can to *step over* it. This leads to a lot of emotional unhealing and wreaks havoc in every area of our life.

Ephesians 6:11 says "Put on the full armor of God so that you can take a stand against the devil's schemes." His schemes are very real. If we ignore them instead of shed light on them, we can end up paralyzed, repeating the same mistakes over and over and end up knee deep in self destructive behaviors. This was me.

But this time I was done. I knew I could face them because this time, I had God (and His armor.) I had truth, righteousness, peace, faith, salvation, prayer, and the Word of God. I was ready to do life different. And with all this in my arsenal, nothing was stopping me.

Journal:

1. Take a moment and say this prayer: "God, are there any old wounds that need healing? Show me all the things you want to make new and I will surrender it all to you. Amen."

2. Now write down all the things the Holy Spirit reveals to you.

_____

_____

_____

_____

_____

_____

_____

_____

_____

Now look over your notes and say this prayer:

> Lord, today I completely surrender all the pain of my past to you. All the ways I've been hurt from childhood to now are yours to heal. Today I will allow myself the pain to feel the hurt and then I will put on your armor of truth, righteousness, faith, peace and salvation. I will go to your Word to fight the lies of the enemy and to comfort me. I will turn to prayer as my sword and to your presence as my safe place. I will no longer allow my past to paralyze me. Instead, I will remember that you call me loved, redeemed, pure, *worthy,* friend and no longer a slave to sin. I am set free! Thank you, Lord, for your love and grace. Amen.

Tuesday- Day 2
Truth over Feelings

Now that you've felt the feelings that you didn't want to face, you have to continue facing them. They will continue to come up in life but now they aren't so scary! You have already gone from believing the lie from the enemy that if you faced them then you'd never come back from it. But as you discovered yesterday, you will! I love the "truth train." Following the truth train all the way till the end reminds you that God has you no matter what. For example, when I got married, I had all this past hurt from old relationships that made me feel like if my husband was unfaithful that I'd just die! Until I learned that I had to take the truth train all the way to the final destination. Beth Moore said it best in a sermon when she said "if my husband cheats then what?!" I'll be devastated. "Ok then what after that?" I'll be so rip roaring mad I won't be able to see straight.

"Ok then what?" Then I'll cry. "Ok then what?" Well I'll wake up the next day and get my kids to school and try to make it through the day. "ok then what?" Then I'll go to church and pray on Sunday and still be hurting. "Ok then what?" Then I'll continue caring for my kids and going to work. "Ok then what?" I'll eventually probably start to feel a bit better and keep going? "Then what?" Then GOD! Ladies, we will turn to God and eventually heal and then maybe get married again or have a beautiful life filled with loving friendships and missions trips and loving our kids! Our life isn't over. Following the truth train allows us to remember we still have God and we will be OKAY! No matter what lie the enemy is feeding us, God grounds us in TRUTH. He has the final say and spoiler alert: he WINS! This is a practice we must make perfect. When these negative feelings come up, we must strengthen that "mind change muscle" and turn to the truth. And eventually it will be a habit that leads us to a free and joyful life in Christ!

Let's have a little fun today. Sometimes we hold these negative feelings in our bodies. So, whatever is weighing you down, bring it top of mind and move your body! Whether you turn on your favorite worship song and dance or take a walk around your neighborhood while you speak truth over the lies, then release them! I have found myself joyfully crying doing this exercise.

Negative Feelings I'm Holding In:

_____

_____

_____

_____

_____

_____

Then end quietly with this prayer:

Lord, you are so good! You have reminded me of what is real and what is not. You have brought me to a place to understand that my feelings aren't so scary once I know your truth! I have released these negative thoughts in mind and body today. I'm so grateful that you have brought me this far and you are only doing "a good work in me that you will bring to completion" like your Word promises in Philippians 1:6. I love you faithfully and endlessly and I'm grateful that you love me the same.

Amen.

Wednesday- Day 3
The Key to Free

For so many years I was a prisoner of my own life. I chose to lock myself in chains that I put myself in. On the outside I may have looked free but in my mind, I was keeping myself in a jail cell of unforgiveness. Everything that ever happened was everyone else's fault. That boyfriend was the problem, that friendship was the problem and so on. I made myself believe that I had nothing to do with my choices and that I was the victim. I identified so much with the victim after my first abusive relationship that it was just comfortable after that and blaming others for my problems was an easy habit. But what I later found is that while it is easy in the moment, it is hard on the soul and does not make for a particularly good life. I needed to let go! I needed to let everyone go that ever hurt me and find forgiveness. And it was not until I felt God's grace that I could find grace for others. What is a grace? The best, most beautiful picture of grace to me is in this verse: "But God demonstrates his love for us in this: that while we were still sinners, Christ died for us." Apply that to you personally now. Think about the worst thing you have ever done to somebody, and right when you tell them what you did, they give up their life and die so that you can live! The moment I realized that God gave me that grace was the moment my whole life changed. Another awesome picture of grace is when Jesus washed his disciple's feet the night before he was crucified knowing that many of them would betray him. Think about that for a second. Back then they wore thin sandals and stepped in all kinds of things! Yet God, Creator and King of everything and everyone, knowingly washed the feet of the same man that would lead the soldiers to him and then hung on a cross. If Jesus can wash the feet of His betrayers, I can forgive my enemies. When I remember that I am the betrayer and that sinner is me, I can forgive.

Have you ever hurt someone and then quickly come up with a reason you should be given grace for it? I know I have. So, if I can do that for myself, I must remember that the other person has a reason too. And when I try to empathize with them in my own mind (even though it can be hard) I can usually get to a place of grace. And that is when I can release it! "Maybe they had a bad day. Maybe their parents treated them horribly as a child. Maybe they witnessed their parents treat each other that way. Maybe they were deeply hurting inside." Although we may never know the reason and never get an apology, I find it so freeing to give them a pass and forgive them. Remember the devil wants us to believe that holding on to the hurt and resentment, protects us. But that is simply not true. In fact, when we release it, is when we are stronger than before and a whole lot happier! After learning this, I have often come up with a great reason that someone hurt me, and they do not even know it! In doing so I can get back to a place of love and no longer live in fear or resentment. I am also no longer the victim and it feels good knowing I have some control over my own life. I hold myself accountable for where I could have done things differently or where I could have chosen differently. Then I forgive myself too because I realize I did the best I could with what I knew and vow to do better next time. You go from victim mentality to a victor mentality and from sad and in chains to freed and forgiven.

Homework: Make a list of the person or people that hurt you and how. Then after that, write next to it a compassion reason. Remember, it may not even be the real reason but being compassionate is exactly what Jesus does for us.

_____

_____

_____

_____

_____

Then when you are finished, look over the list and say this prayer:

Lord, I know they are hurting too, and I choose to be compassionate. I choose to forgive them and myself for what happened. We both are free and forgiven by your precious blood that you shed on the cross for us. You have forgiven them in the same way you have forgiven me. Thank you. Amen.

Thursday- Day 4
A Better Way to Live

Do you remember as a kid, playing on that rusty metal merry go round that just spun around? Some kids stood on it holding on to the bars, while other kids pushed it around. Many kids would stay on it no matter how dizzy it made them, and other kids would jump off when they got dizzy enough. Well, if we are going to use this as a metaphor for life, I was the kid that stayed on way too long. I let the external forces continue to push me and was not brave enough to take the jump. Until "that day."

I'll never forget the day I decided that I was no longer going to live the way I was living. I could no longer take the dizziness. Toxic relationship. Break up. Broken heart. Party Hard. Repeat. It was killing me. Literally. But now the dizziness was worse than the fear of facing my pain. I felt like I had no choice but to be brave, so I jumped! I stopped the cycle of self-destruction and surrendered to "feeling." I was committed to change. And with an open heart and a willingness to do whatever it took; I was led to everything I needed. From people to songs, books and church, the Holy Spirit was guiding me. "For all who are being led by the Spirit of God, these are sons and daughters of God" - Romans 8:24. Living life my way did nothing but harm me. I thought I was in control, but I was so wrong. Holding on to that bar tight while spinning gives us a sense of control. But little do we know, on the other side of that, if we let go and give our life to God, we can stop spinning in circles. We can let something bigger than ourselves guide us. He is a God of wisdom. "But when He, the Spirit of truth, comes, He will guide you into all the truth; for He will not speak on His own initiative, but whatever He hears, He will speak; and He will disclose to you what is to come." John 16:13. He will lead us into TRUTH and disclose what is to come! Guys! God is wisdom. I was 31 years old and living a life of stupidity to put it bluntly. Fast forward to today, and I get comments on my blog posts that say something to the effect of "you are wise beyond your years" from women that are much older than me. But the truth is, it is not my wisdom. It is just that I decided to listen to that "still, small voice" (1 Kings 19:12). I was finally allowing the Holy Spirit to take over and put me on a path to a better way to live.

Are you on a cycle? Do you need to jump off the merry go round?

Below write addictive behaviors that might be showing up in your life. When you feel fear how do you respond? Alcohol, a bad relationship, food, numbing out on social media?

_____

_____

_____

_____

_____

_____

_____

_____

_____

_____

_____

_____

_____

_____

If you are ready to let go of your fears and jump off the cycle you are on and into the arms of the Holy Spirit, make a commitment to this bible verse anytime you reach for the things that keep you on the merry go round:

"I do not have a spirit of fear, but of power, and of love and of a sound mind." 2 Tim. 1:7

Friday- Day 5
Relationships are Remedies

Once we decide to make changes and let the Holy Spirit lead, we often are guided to do things we never thought we'd do or even could do! I didn't think I could be alone. I was in a relationship from the time I was 14 and now that I had committed to a new way of life, the Holy Spirit made it very clear to me that it was time to face my fears of being "alone." Not only was he saying, "don't date and make Jesus your boyfriend", He also made it clear that I was to live alone. Growing up in a house full of kids and then living with my boyfriends, I had no clue how to do this and wasn't even sure I could. How was I going to do it physically, emotionally, and financially? But the Spirit kept telling me I could do it and I needed it for healing. So I took my next leap of faith. Scared and excited I was alone in every sense of the word, but I don't remember ever a time in my life where I felt more fulfilled. I obeyed what

God told me and I began a rewarding healing journey. I went through a year of learning who Christ is and who I am in Christ. It was wonderful. But I was not getting any younger and I felt the Lord tell me after a year that I was ready. He had someone for me. But he wanted me to be alert, disciplined and follow His nudge. It was so clear when someone was not for me. In the past, I would have ignored the red flags and given these men many more chances to "prove me wrong." But at the very first nudge from the Holy Spirit when it was not right, I obeyed and cut it off kindly. And that obedience eventually led me to my husband. Praise God. But little did I know how HARD it would still be even when a relationship was ordained by God. Two people with their own emotional past and scars, coming together was going to take work that I had not fully recognized.

At first, I didn't recognize that my marriage was making me better. I was upset that we weren't just smooth sailing. But because I was surrounded by people who led their life with

Christ and I continued persevering in my own spiritual walk, God made it clear to me that this was what marriage was for. Living alone was easy. No one was telling me how I "hurt their feelings" or that I "could have said that nicer." But my marriage reflected me. It was showing me who I was when I was not in the best mood or when I wasn't being the person God intended me to be. And the devil takes full advantage of that. He wants to make us believe that it is the other person. And at first, I put it all on my husband. Heck, I still get caught doing that now! Remember yesterday when I said that I followed that "still small voice?" Well, the devil speaks first and loudest and often that has led me to responding wrong. However now with that knowledge, I can take a step back even during a heated argument and remember that I play a part in the situation. I ask that still small voice for help. And I learn to look at the situation with grace, forgiveness, and compassion. Relationships are the remedy to look more like Jesus.

Journal Work:

Think about the relationship you are currently struggling with. Is there something in there that may reflect your own insecurities or scars? This is not a time to beat yourself up but instead to use it to grow and look more like Christ. For example, when my husband would tell me I was talking harshly, I would defend myself and say, "well you don't always talk nice to me either." Here is a chance where I can write down and address my own behavior. I might write "I'm going to make a conscious effort to speak loving to my husband when I'm bothered because that's how I want him to treat me."

_____

_____

_____

_____

_____

_____

_____

_____

_____

_____

_____

_____

_____

Then pray over your journal time: Lord, thank you for showing me in my relationships how to look more like you. Relationships are sacred. And I'm so grateful for the people you've blessed me with. Thank you again. Let me honor these relationships and let me glorify who you are in them. I ask you this in your Holy name. Amen

Week 2

Monday- Day 1
Misplaced Idols

We ended last week on relationships. So, since we are on the subject, let's dive into how the devil can really wreak havoc on our lives if we've misplaced our ideas around them. This could be a friendship, a boyfriend, husband, a child and even on our parents. It wasn't until I started to ask God to show me where I was failing in my romantic relationships that I finally saw what I was doing wrong. I wasn't looking for a man to compliment me, I was looking for a man to complete me and be my source of happiness. But Gods still small voice whispered, "only I can do that." No person or thing outside ourselves can make us happy. Sure, they all have their benefits and bring us moments of happiness throughout our lives. But they cannot be what we base our joy on. For example, if you make your husband your idol, if he is in a bad mood than guess what? You will also be in a bad mood. When we make something imperfect the meter for our happiness, we are in for a looooong ride. And if one day they are gone, then we too will feel we have no reason to go on. And we know that if there is breath in our lungs, then God's purpose for our lives remains.

Now obviously our kids and our husbands can be things that we call our "pride and joy", but they can't be our HOPE. They are not the answers to all life's problems. And they will let us down…more than once! But there is a perfect being that we can put our full hope and trust in. *There is only one.* Only one place our souls can find perfect peace.

"I depend on God alone. I put my hope in Him. He alone saves and protects me. He is my defender, and I will never be defeated. My salvation and honor depend on Him. He is my strong protector; He is my shelter. Trust in God at all times. Tell Him all your troubles for He is our refuge."– Psalm 62:5-8

My life changed the day I put all my hope in Him. Even now when the devil tries to feed me a fearful thought and I think of something happening to my children or even in my marriage, I am soon reminded that with God I have everything I need. Of course, it doesn't mean I wouldn't be heartbroken, but it does mean that my life would still have so much purpose because I live for God alone. Every hard moment I have ever faced, I've seen His faithful hand turn it into something beautiful. And I know He will never let me down.

Journal: Is there someone in your life you are putting a lot of pressure on? That is usually the first sign that they are a misplaced idol in your life. When you can freely let people just be themselves, is the moment you know they have the proper place in your life and heart. The King of our hearts should be Jesus Christ.

_____

_____

_____

_____

_____

_____

_____

_____

Prayer: God, you are perfect in all your ways and for that we praise your name! Please show us where we are putting people as idols in our lives and help us put You there instead. We know that is Your rightful place. We surrender everyone we love to you. We trust you will take care of them. And we know that the greatest relationship we have in our lives is the one we have with you. All our hope is in you. We love You. Amen.

Tuesday- Day 2
That Special Someone

L et us continue today with idols. It's clear in the Old Testament that over and over again God told the people to "crush their idols" or He would do it for them. This was so important to God. So, if it's important to God than it's important to me. I'm sure the same goes for you. And I know us women especially could use some help in the area of love. Yes. You and I both know we tend to idolize that L word. Whether it's with a boyfriend or a husband, we can easily put them on a pedestal where only One belongs. Now I'm not discounting the fact that we are to honor our husbands. We absolutely are. Nor am I saying we shouldn't make our marriage the second most important relationship there is to God. Because we should. But there is a fine line between honor and idolatry.

At first we may think "no way! I do NOT idolize him." But idolatry can be sneaky. It's sin and it's from the devil. And anything from the devil is sneaky. Let's start here:

Be honest. Many times we can put a lot of pressure on our men to fulfill us. And if they don't, then they are in big trouble. And many times, they don't even know it. Lol. As we read yesterday, God is the only one who can satisfy our souls. But sometimes we need to do some work to let this one sink in. The only thing that we should be holding tightly to is Jesus.

When we make our men our "source", we are letting the devil lead. And when we let the devil lead, we allow him to deceive us with false illusions about our partner. But as soon as we let the Holy Spirit lead, we are reminded that we are whole in Christ. And when we are whole in Christ, we aren't looking to a person to complete us and this is where we find our relationship at its best and its healthiest.

One thing I did to take notice of how I treated my husband like an idol was in how I responded. For example, I had set up a lunch with a friend and the morning of she texted me and said she was sorry, but she didn't get much sleep and she was really hoping we could reschedule. I told her I totally understood, and we set up lunch for the following week. Had my husband done the same thing, at that time I would have given him the silent treatment or really taken him on a guilt trip. The devil wants nothing more than to ruin marriage. And viewing my husband as an idol instead of a friend that I love, the devil separates us. If I'm being honest, I'm still learning how to navigate this one. But I have learned some things along the way that have made a huge difference.

First, I remind myself that my husband isn't the only light in my life.

Colossians 2:10- "And you have been made complete in Christ, who is the head of all rule and authority."

1. Make a list of people that fill your cup when you are with them. (Family, friends, kids etc.)

2. Make a list of things you love doing. (Exercising, reading, sitting with God, and journaling about it, listening to a podcast, music etc.)

_____

_____

_____

_____

_____

_____

_____

_____

_____

_____

_____

_____

_____

_____

_____

_____

_____

Now keep this list on hand. Whenever the devil tries to convince us that love only comes in the form of our husbands or boyfriends, prove him wrong and switch on one of our other light switches. Pray this prayer and then go call a friend or go exercise! And then give your man a big hug after and tell him how much you love him. The devil will not even have foothold!

Lord,

You have made me complete in you. You are my main source and you have blessed me with so many wonderful sources of joy. I want to come to my husband complete in You and not make him solely responsible for my joy. Please recall all the things you have given me that bring light to my life and then let me release my husband to love me freely and me do the same to him.

Amen.

Wednesday, Day 3
Every Thought Counts

"We take every thought captive and make it obey Christ." 2 Corinithians 10:5b

It took me a long time to realize that I was letting my mind rule my life. My thoughts were completely undisciplined, and I would spin out of control down a rabbit hole of worry, fear and anxiety. I have heard it said that "worry is a prayer for chaos." And I don't know about you, but I certainly don't want to be praying *for* chaos! But that is exactly what I was doing. Especially in my 20's. Since then, I have gotten a lot better at disciplining my mind and recognizing when the devil is having a field day in there. The focus of today is to show the importance of conquering the devils schemes of feeding us negative thoughts and learning to 'take captive every thought' by recalling God's truth. Disciples are disciplined- hence the name. And it all starts in our mind.

Let's crack open our Bibles and see how God wants us to think. Yes, crazy enough, our thoughts are so important to God that He made it clear in scripture what we should think about. We will start with Philippians 4:8: "Finally, brothers and sisters, whatever is *true*, whatever is *noble*, whatever is *right*, whatever *is pure*, whatever is *lovely*, whatever is *admirable*—if anything is *excellent* or *praiseworthy*—**think about such things.**"

Whenever my thoughts don't align with what is true, noble, right, pure, lovely, admirable, excellent or praiseworthy, I do my best to quickly acknowledge it. Each day the devil is waiting to pull you down to his level, but the Holy Spirit is right there to remind you of truth and pull you back up! Remember we "do not have a spirit of fear or timidity but one of peace, love, power and a **sound mind**." Reciting both of these verses in scripture will have you back on track to letting the Spirit lead. Have you ever noticed that when the devil is having a field day with your thoughts, it seems like one bad thing after the next happens? For example, you wake up late and it triggers your negative thinking. You stop for coffee because you didn't have time for breakfast after your shower and there is only one person working the register at the coffee shop. You get to work late, and you find out your boss called a meeting. The rest of the day you are scared he's going to call you into his office. You quietly slip out the door at 5 in fear and head home. Once you get there, you start responding to everyone you love negatively. Everyone is upset and you end the night in tears. That pattern could have been stopped much earlier in the day if you rebuked the devil and realigned yourself with the Holy Spirit. And this just doesn't stop with our days. This goes into months and years. Our minds are powerful, and our thoughts shape who we are and what we will become. We have much more power than we give ourselves credit for. We were made in God's image and given power and authority. And **when we change our mind, we change our life.** Here are some God breathed verses that remind us of this truth:

"Change your mind" is the main theme of Jesus' first sermon (Matt. 4:17 AMP). "From that time Jesus began to preach and say, repent (change your inner self- your old way of thinking, regret past sins, live your life in a way that proves repentance and seek God's purpose for your life,) for the kingdom of heaven is at hand."

Another verse in scripture says,

"As someone thinks within himself, so he is."- Proverbs 23:7. This verse plain and simply says that what you choose to think determines your reality. You have the power to change your reality by shifting your thoughts.

Let's start today with How?

Step One: Take notice. To become disciplined, we have to first take notice of our negative thoughts. We may have never even realized how many negative thoughts we were having until we do this exercise. When we shine light on the devil, he flees.

Step Two: Rebuke the thought. For example, let's stick with the story from earlier. If we wake up late thinking "great I'm late and it's going to be an awful day and my boss is going to give the third degree," quickly say "I rebuke that thought by the blood of Jesus." Suddenly something powerful happens. Just like Jesus rebuked Satan when he was trying to tempt him, we must do the same thing. When we take this step, we quickly disassociate with the bad thought and reconnect with the Holy Spirit.

Step 3: Replace the thought. This is where we "change our mind." When we woke up late, we take that negative thought captive and switch it to something *lovely* like "I woke up late and got some extra rest that I must have needed. I'll forego my breakfast and have a cup of coffee when I get to the office and just have a really great lunch!" When we are in panic mode or fear mode, we don't think with clarity. Staying focused on the good (like phil.4:8 tells us too) helps our decision making and leads us in a better direction.

Today take this action and write down each step and how it affected you. Continue with this as long as you feel the need.

_____

_____

_____

_____

_____

_____

_____

_____

_____

_____

Prayer for today:

Dear Lord,

Help me fix my eyes on you. You are all those things described in Philippians: true, noble, right, pure, lovely, admirable, excellent, and praiseworthy. Whenever I'm tempted to let the devil lead, quickly help me reconnect with your truth, letting the Spirit lead me. Help me take captive every thought and make it obedient to you. Your Word says that "As someone thinks within himself, so he is." Keep my thoughts disciplined and keep them in line with your way. Amen.

Thursday- Day 4
"And do not give the devil a foothold"

We are coming into the end of the second week of this journey. We've done a lot of digging deep and transforming our thoughts and old ways. But many times, when the devil knows we are on a godly path, he revs up his schemes and attacks harder than before. In fact, I notice the devil tries twice as hard with me now that I am a Christian then when I was living a life of sin. I was already doing the devils work back then so he had no reason to attack me. "Calling out" the devil, if you will, is always the best way to make him flee. So, lets clearly identify some of the main ways he attacks.

1. Fear- As soon as we start to do well in an area, many times the devil tries to knock us back down with fear. For example, you know God has placed it on your heart to

start dating again. As soon as you start dating someone the devil says things like "he's too good to be true."

2. Guilt- God made it clear to you that he wants you to take care of yourself and the body he gave you because you are the dwelling place for the Holy Spirit. He gave you that body and he wants you to be good to it so that you can be used for Kingdom purposes for a long time while on the earth. You do great every day until you didn't get to a workout and then guilt has you in a tizzy, so you eat bad that day too. This completely separates you from God and the devil has you right where he wants you. And he wants to further that separation days on end.

3. Attacking others- the devil makes us believe that if we project our guilt or fear on others then we are protected. So as soon as your relationship is going well for example and the devil feeds you fear, you then attack your partner about the fear.

This not only causes chaos, but it also keeps you stuck in your old ways and patterns.

So now that we know the devil's schemes, what can we do to protect ourselves from them?

"11 Put on the full armor of God, so that you can take your stand against the devil's schemes. 12 For our struggle is not against flesh and blood, but against the rulers, against the authorities, against the powers of this dark world and against the spiritual forces of evil in the heavenly realms. 13 Therefore put on the full armor of God, so that when the day of evil comes, you may be able to stand your ground, and after you have done everything, to stand. 14 Stand firm then, with the belt of truth buckled around your waist, with the breastplate of righteousness in place, 15 and with your feet fitted with the readiness that comes from the gospel of peace."
– Eph. 6: 11-15

We must equip ourselves with the truth of God. And that is in His Word and in Prayer. Here is how I personally have done this in my life on a daily basis:

I start my day with prayer and in the Word for at least 30 minutes. In this time, I listen to a few worship songs to get my heart in the place it should always be, praising my Savior. After that I journal my thanksgiving and prayers to God. Then I read the Word or a devotional and in my journal, I write down everything that stood out to me and I ask God to help me live it out.

As the day goes on, I try to check in on my thoughts. And ask God to change my mind (repent) where I have allowed the devil to interfere.

Then at night, I get in bed with my journal and start writing and praying. I do my best to recognize all the places I need forgiveness and who I need to forgive and pray for God's help with both. I then write down anyone then needs special prayers. And lastly, I write down all the things I am thankful for that day and I get to close my eyes with a thankful heart.

This is the best way I know how to not give the devil a foothold in my own life. You are welcome to try my way and tweak it in a way that works best for you!

_____

_____

_____

_____

_____

_____

_____

_____

_____

_____

_____

_____

_____

_____

_____

_____

_____

_____

Now let's end this day with a prayer!

Lord, You are so good. You remind us that the dark will never overcome the light. And with your truth we will always be victorious over the wicked schemes of the devil. Show me the best way to personally protect myself from the devil. And help me on this journey to do so. I know you are with me every step of the way. Thank You. And I love You. Amen.

Friday Day 5
Proverbs 23:7

"As someone thinks within himself, so he is."-
Proverbs 23:7.

I mentioned this verse two days ago and today it's one we are going to focus on and apply even further.

Before the Holy Spirit got a hold of me, I didn't think much of myself. In fact, I was just the culmination of what people said I was. I believed everything everyone said about me. That ranged from really positive things to really negative things, depending on who said it. The biggest lesson I have learned on this journey is that *I am who God says I am!* And if you read scripture and understand all the things God says you are, you will instantly be transformed. If I believe scripture, then I also believe who He says I am and that rolls over into every area of my life now. Here is what he says about you too:

<u>Accepted</u>- Receive one another, then, just as Christ also received you, to God's glory (Romans 15:7).

<u>A Temple</u>- Do you not know that you are God's temple and that God's Spirit lives in you (1 Corinthians 6:19)?

<u>Righteous</u>- God made the one who did not know sin to be sin for us, so that in him we would become the righteousness of God (2 Corinthians 5:21).

<u>Blessed</u>- Blessed is the God and Father of our Lord Jesus Christ, who has blessed us with every spiritual blessing in the heavenly realms in Christ (Ephesians 1:3)

<u>Chosen, Holy, and Blameless</u>- For he chose us in Christ before the foundation of the world that we may be holy and unblemished in his sight in love (Ephesians 1:4).

<u>Redeemed and Forgiven</u>- In him we have redemption through his blood, the forgiveness of

our trespasses, according to the riches of his grace (Ephesians 1:7).

Complete- "You have been filled in him, who is the head over every ruler and authority (Colossians 2:10)."

And these are just to name a few…

Are you living this way? Do you believe these things about yourself?

Change can happen in an instant when you change your mind. You can go from someone who sees yourself as a worrier to a warrior. You can go from believing you are unworthy to worthy when you adopt and align yourself with God's thinking.

Do you see yourself as lazy and unworthy of a good job title? Do you see yourself as unlovable and not worthy of a good marriage? God disagrees! You are both worthy and loved!

All it took was the desire to change my perception and willingness to follow the Holy Spirit that led me to a much better way of life.

Homework:

1. Who do you believe you are? Who do you see yourself as? What are some things other people have said about you that you have let grow deep roots inside?

_____

_____

_____

_____

_____

_____

_____

_____

2. Who do you want to be? What do you want to accomplish?

_____

_____

_____

_____

_____

_____

_____

_____

_____

_____

3. Write a statement that realigns your thinking with God's thinking using the answers from the questions above. For example: I used to think I wasn't worthy of love, but I wanted to be married so badly. I used to think I wasn't that intelligent, and everything rested on what

I looked like. But God said I am worthy; I am loved and I have His wisdom that he reveals to me daily! So, my new statement became:

"I am a woman worthy of love and marriage. My Husband calls me precious. I am a writer and teacher of good things. God has equipped me with everything I need to be successful in all areas."

_____

_____

_____

_____

_____

_____

_____

_____

_____

_____

_____

_____

_____

_____

_____

_____

_____

_____

_____

Once you have written your statement, read over it, pray over it and let the Holy Spirit encourage you daily as you remind yourself of it.

Week 3

Monday- Day 1
"We Walk By Faith, Not By Sight"

If you've ever read the New Testament or at least parts of it, you saw Jesus often tell people who were once in trouble to "go, your faith has saved you" or "now you are healed, your faith has made you well." When he spoke to them, he was also speaking to us. Ladies, focused faith is our road map in life. When we surrender to faith in God, the Holy Spirit is our guide, and we find ourselves saved from an awful situation. But there are also times in life we allow doubt and fear to rule our minds and we totally miss the way we are supposed to take. We unintentionally block ourselves from good things that God has for us because we are consumed with the lies of the devil and the anxiety of our flesh. But when we have focused faith, we can clearly hear the Holy Spirit and rebuke all of it.

We never wonder if the sun will come up because we have faith that it will. Right? That same faith can be part of every moment of our lives. But we need to do our part. For example, say you are in a job you hate. Are you so focused on the job you hate that you miss the job that you are seeking right in front of you? When we live by faith, we are led by love. And when we are led by love, God leads us to focus on the right things.

Today let's take an inventory on the things we have yet to surrender in faith in our lives. Do you hate your job? Are you in any conflict in any of your relationships? Are you struggling in your finances? Etc...

_____

_____

_____

_____

_____

_____

_____

_____

_____

_____

_____

_____

_____

Now that you have your list draw a line down the middle. And on the opposite side write the words "Faith Affirmation." Here is your chance to let the Holy Spirit lead you with loving thoughts over what you are going through. You will be led in truth and as you do this day after day in these particular areas you will become more disciplined with your thoughts in these areas and the Spirit will little by little show you the way. So for example, let's take finances... If you wrote "Financial Struggle" on the opposite side of the line you will instead have faith over the issue and write something like "I spend my money wisely. I have all that I need. God provides for me abundantly." Now I want you to do this with each of your struggles then tape your affirmations to your mirror. These are little faith prayers that you will say each day as you surrender your struggles to God knowing he will provide.

Philipians 4:19- And my God will supply every need of yours according to his riches in glory in Christ Jesus.

Lord, we know that we have not fully surrendered every circumstance in our life to you. We repent and ask for your forgiveness and for the strength to have focused faith. We want to hear your voice above lies. We want to see all our situations with love and truth from the Spirit so we can be led to do everything your way. We love you and are so grateful that you have shown us to walk by faith and not by sight. Amen.

Tuesday- Day 2
"She is clothed in strength and dignity and laughs without fear of the future"

After yesterday's confirmation of faith in all areas of your life, now I'm sure you can see how the Proverbs 31 woman had strength, dignity and a joyful outlook on the future without fear.

Many of us have spent our lives wishing, hoping, and praying but not fully having faith in God's way for our lives. It's a struggle for all of us! Even those of us who know God's way. That's why being disciplined and in hot pursuit of Christ is so important. That's why he tells us to do these things "without ceasing" and to "remain in Him." How disciplined are you today in your spiritual walk with God? Do you set aside time morning and night to start and end your day with the One who gave you the day? Do you periodically check in with Him and send up prayers throughout the day? Or read books and podcasts to firm up your foundation in Christ?

When you are strong in the Lord you are clothed in strength. When you *know* whose hands hold your future, you can laugh without fear of it. But *knowing* takes work

Let us take a minute to rate our spiritual lives from one to ten. One being the worst and ten being the best. Is there room for improvement? Then write down how you will be more disciplined this year and put it on your daily calendar as if it's an appointment you can't miss. Because honestly, appointments with the One who gave us this life, are the ones we need to show up for the most. He can give you the answers that no one else can and provide like no one else will. Right now, you may not have the full faith of "knowing" that God is *for you*. But that is why this exercise and the implementation of it is so important. The more you sit with God and discover who he is, the more your relationship with Him develops, and you will have the trust you need. You will see Him show up in ways that you never imagined and it will lead you to a strong faith where fear doesn't nearly have the hold on you that it used to. And I'm certain if we just keep showing up in this way, one day we can live with no fear at all.

_____

_____

_____

Lord, I want nothing more than to be a Proverbs 31 woman. I want the dignity, strength, and fearless future that she has. I know this is the woman you made me to be. I know the enemy daily tries his best to make me weak and does all he can to make me fall off track, but today I am making a commitment to be a disciplined disciple of You, Your Word, and Your Way. Please give me the courage and grace to this. We ask you these things Jesus, in your Holy Name. Amen

Wednesday- Day 3
Co-Creating with God

"We don't choose what we will do for God; He invites us to join Him where He wants to involve us."

— Henry T. Blackaby, Experiencing God

This is where it gets exciting. I remember once I had worked through so much emotional muck, did the hard work of being alone and just surrendering so much to Jesus and letting God change me, I was ready to jump in with Him and really *do life.*

I wanted to do His Will for my life and choose what He wanted for me. But I also knew that if I had desires in my heart, that He was the one that gave them to me. I had a mentor who really helped me along this journey, and I am SO THANKFUL that God put her in my life. If you don't have a mentor from your church, I highly recommend getting one! But that's a story for another day. Anyway, she knew how much I desired a husband and children. She told me she too thought I was ready to start dating and she suggested I write a letter to God about my husband. She made it very clear not to focus on the framework but get really detailed about his character and the man I thought God would want for me. She told me anytime I got lonely to read the letter and feel hope rise.

Ladies do not be afraid to ask God for what you want. *Matthew 7:7-8: "Ask and it will be given to you; seek and you will find; knock and the door will be opened to you.* He wants to give you your desires. Just like you want to give your children theirs!

I know it can seem selfish and even sometimes "new age" to ask God for desires and believe that He will give them to you but think of him as a father! He wants us to go to Him for *everything.*

So, what happened with the letter you may be wondering? Well, I'd say God gave me about 90% of what I asked for and the other 10% was MORE than I could have ever imagined. After meeting my husband, two week later I knew he was it. The *verse Ephesians 3:20- "Now to him who is able to do immeasurably more than all we ask or imagine, according to his power that is at work within us"* just echoed in my mind as I got to know him. The other awesome thing about writing that letter was that when someone would come along and I'd go on a date with them, it was so clear when that man wasn't it and I wasted so much less time than the 10 years previous I had given to men. If we ask God for our desires, get really clear with Him about them and make sure we are looking less at the framework and more at what we feel God wants for us, then we can co-create with Him and accomplish His will for our lives. And the outcome is better than we could even imagine ourselves. It may not always look the way we thought it would (for example, I never imagined marrying a man with 3 children and having to move to another state) but it's always what is best for us.

Homework: Co- create your life with God. What are some of the things you haven't taken to God? Are there desires you have that you haven't asked God what he wants those to look like? Take your desires to him. Get really focused and then write Him a letter. Be focused on what you want but open to all the possibilities that He wants for you! This is the fun part. It's you and God. Let Him lead the way.

_____

_____

_____

_____

_____

_____

_____

Thursday- Day 4
Invite Him In

When you began this journey, I'm not sure what you had in mind. Maybe you thought that you would learn more about the Bible or of God? While I hope you learned about those things some, I also hope you realize that the most important thing of all this is your RELATIONSHIP. This was to set you on a path to get into a deep relationship with your loving Father and surrender it all to Him. He craves relationship with you more than anything. Get into the Word and into Bible Studies but the action step after that must always be taken. Take your knowledge into your experiences and let Him lead.

This doesn't stop at your prayer time. Or church on Sundays. He wants you to invite him into your dreams, struggles, marriage, healthy, home etc. We are women that face real everyday choices, and we have to invite God into them if we want to live the best life He has for us.

Sometimes when I'm driving in the car alone, I reach over to the passenger side with an open hand and pretend Jesus is holding it. Yes, I know this sounds crazy! But I know Jesus loves when I do it. This is a divine romance. He is in love with me and I'm in love with Him. And the same is true for you. Sometimes our partner isn't always going to be able to fulfill every need and we shouldn't expect him to! But God ALWAYS does. If I'm lonely, and I take his hand, it immediately puts a smile on my face. I turn up my worship music and we have deep and intimate conversation that my soul needs. When you look at God this way, as your one true love and best friend, you will do life that way too. Try it! It is the most important relationship we have. Shouldn't we tell Him how in love we are with Him? Shouldn't we spew all the mushy ways we feel about Him to Him? This only strengthens a relationship!

Homework: What are some ways you can enjoy your relationship with Jesus more? How can you show him you are committed to him? How can you tell him all the ways you love him in a way that seems silly but is the way you show love best?

_____

_____

_____

_____

_____

_____

_____

_____

_____

_____

_____

Friday- Day 5
Worthy

Well, we did it. 3 weeks of deep, spiritual work of surrender, forgiveness, love and letting the Holy Spirit lead. I'm so proud of you. This work wasn't easy. Maybe you got emotional or mad or maybe you were just ready to get to work and you were excited each day. Either way, I pray that whatever you felt, it led you to a place you have never gone with God and with an outlook that *with God all things are possible.*

When everything changed for me those years ago, I had a strong desire to do life differently. God knew I was ready to receive His message of grace. It didn't matter to Him how bad I messed up and how shameful I had been. He still decided, on my worse day, that I was *worthy* of suffering and dying for. In my ugliest, meanest, most sinful place, he still didn't want heaven without me. So, he took the beatings, the agony, the mocking, and the hanging so that I would one day return to Him.

Because of His grace, I wake up each day, more dedicated then the last, to see life through the light of the Holy Spirit. I will never turn my back on the one who paid it all for me.

I hope you now feel worthy. Worthy of all the goodness that God can bring. Worthy enough to share this knowledge with one who may not feel worthy. It's time to shine God's glory and help others do the same.

Now, I leave you with this to carry with you:

"Our deepest fear is not that we are inadequate. Our deepest fear is that we are powerful beyond measure. It is our light, not our darkness that most frightens us. We ask ourselves, Who am I to be brilliant, gorgeous, talented, fabulous? Actually, Who are you not to be? You are a child of God. Your playing small does not serve the world. There is nothing enlightened about shrinking so that other people won't feel insecure around you. We are all meant to shine, as children do. We were born to make manifest the glory of God that is within us. It's not just in some of us, it's in everyone. And as we let our own light shine, we unconsciously give other people permission to do the same. As we are liberated from our own fear, our presence automatically liberated others. "h

— MARIANNE WILLIAMSON

THE END

Made in the USA
Middletown, DE
02 February 2021

32979084R00066